John Brimhall

Popular CHORD ENCYCLOPEDIA

Written, Edited, Arranged and Produced by John Brimhall
Typography by Maestro Music, Inc., Orem, Utah
Art by James Shaffer

© 1968 (Renewed 1996) BRIMHALL EDUCATIONAL MUSIC, INC. and WARNER BROS. PUBLICATIONS U.S. INC.
This Edition © 1997 BRIMHALL EDUCATIONAL MUSIC, INC. and WARNER BROS. PUBLICATIONS U.S. INC.
All Rights Reserved including Public Performance for Profit

WARNER BROS. PUBLICATIONS - THE GLOBAL LEADER IN PRINT
USA: 15800 NW 48th Avenue, Miami, FL 33014

WARNER/CHAPPELL MUSIC

CANADA: 85 SCARSDALE ROAD, SUITE 101
DON MILLS, ONTARIO, M3B 2R2
SCANDINAVIA: P.O. BOX 533, VENDEVAGEN 85 B
S-182 15, DANDERYD, SWEDEN
AUSTRALIA: P.O. BOX 353
3 TALAVERA ROAD, NORTH RYDE N.S.W. 2113

NUOVA CARISCH

ITALY: VIA M.F. QUINTILIANO 40
20138 MILANO
SPAIN: MAGALLANES, 25
28015 MADRID

INTERNATIONAL MUSIC PUBLICATIONS LIMITED

ENGLAND: SOUTHEND ROAD,
WOODFORD GREEN, ESSEX IG8 8HN
FRANCE: 25 RUE DE HAUTEVILLE, 75010 PARIS
GERMANY: MARSTALLSTR. 8, D-80539 MUNCHEN
DENMARK: DANMUSIK, VOGNMAGERGADE 7
DK 1120 KOBENHAVNK

CHORD CONSTRUCTION

Chords are built of only two standard building blocks—the Major 3rd with 4 half-steps, and the minor 3rd with 3 half steps.

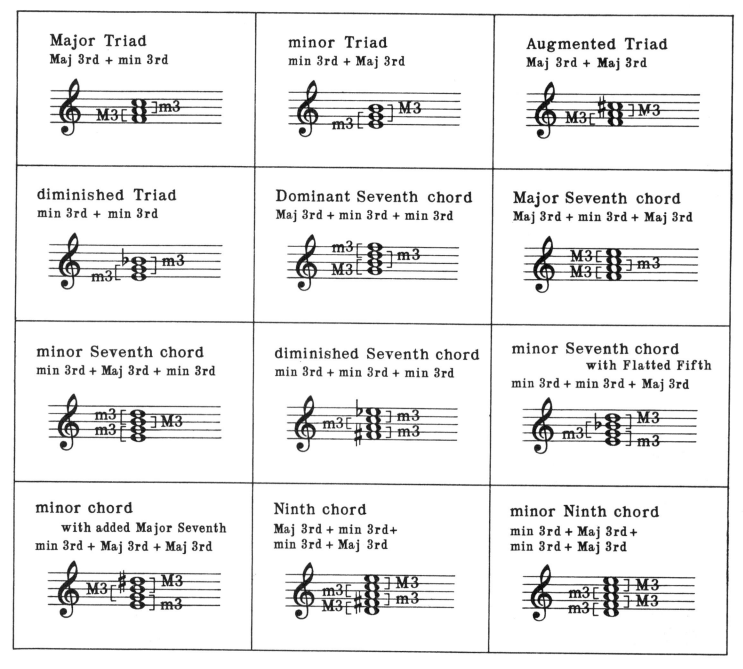

TABLE OF COMPLETE CHORD TYPES (on C)

C Major Triad C	**C minor Triad** Cm	**C diminished Triad** Cdim or C°	**C augmented Triad** Caug or C+	**C Major Triad** with added 6th (C Sixth) C6
C minor Triad with added 6th (C minor 6th) Cm6	**C Major Triad** with Flatted 5th C(♭5)	**C Seventh** C7	**C minor Seventh** Cm7	**C diminished Seventh** Cdim7
C Major Seventh C Maj7	**C Seventh** with Sharp 5th C7♯5	**C Seventh** with Flatted 5th C7♭5	**C Seventh** with Suspended 4th C7(sus)	**C Major Seventh** with Sharp 5th C Maj7♯5
C minor Seventh with Flatted 5th Cm7♭5	**C minor** with raised 7th Cm(♮7)	**C Ninth** C9	**C Ninth** with Sharp 5th C9♯5	**C Seventh** with Flat 9th C7♭9
C Ninth with Flat 5th C9♭5	**C Seventh** with Sharp 9th C7♯9	**C minor Ninth** Cm9	**C Major Seventh** with added 9th C Maj7(add 9)	**C Eleventh** C11
C Thirteenth C13	**C Thirteenth** with Flat 9th C13(♭9)	**C augmented Eleventh** Caug 11	**C Major Triad** with added 6th and 9th C 6/9	**C minor Triad** with added 6th and 9th Cm6/9
C Seventh with Sharp 5th and Flatted 9th C7♯5,♭9	**C Seventh** with Sharp 5th and Sharp 9th C7♯5,♯9	**C minor Ninth** with Flatted 5th Cm9(♭5)	**C Thirteenth** with Sharp 11th C13(♯11)	

C

Key of C Major

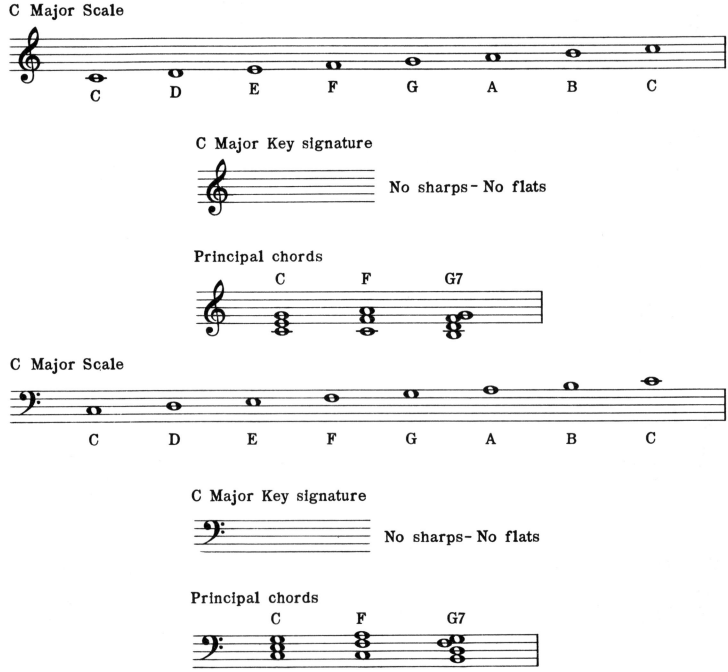

C Major Scale

C D E F G A B C

C Major Key signature

No sharps - No flats

Principal chords

C   F   G7

C Major Scale

C D E F G A B C

C Major Key signature

No sharps - No flats

Principal chords

C   F   G7

Key of D♭ Major

(Same Sound as C♯ Major with 7 sharps)

D♭ Major Scale

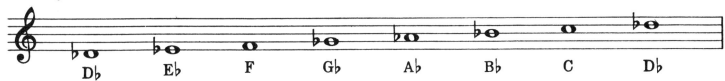

D♭   E♭   F   G♭   A♭   B♭   C   D♭

D♭ Major Key signature

5♭'s— B♭, E♭, A♭, D♭ & G♭

Principal chords

D♭   G♭   A♭7

C♯ Major Key signature

7♯'s— F♯, C♯, G♯, D♯, A♯, E♯ & B♯

Principal chords

C♯   F♯   G♯7

D♭ Major Scale

D♭   E♭   F   G♭   A♭   B♭   C   D♭

D♭ Major Key signature

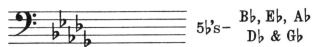

5♭'s— B♭, E♭, A♭ D♭ & G♭

Principal chords

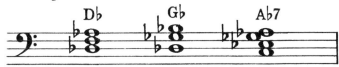

D♭   G♭   A♭7

C♯ Major Key signature

7♯'s— F♯, C♯, G♯, D♯, A♯, E♯ & B♯

Principal chords

C♯   F♯   G♯7

D Key of D Major

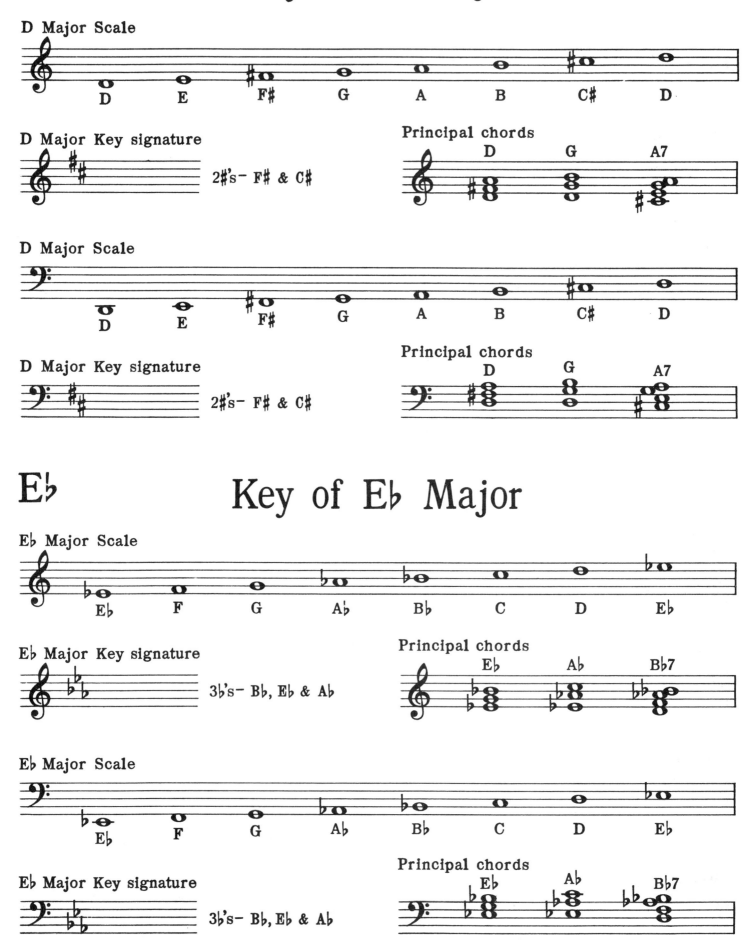

D Major Scale

D E F♯ G A B C♯ D

D Major Key signature

2♯'s— F♯ & C♯

Principal chords

D G A7

D Major Scale

D E F♯ G A B C♯ D

D Major Key signature

2♯'s— F♯ & C♯

Principal chords

D G A7

E♭ Key of E♭ Major

E♭ Major Scale

E♭ F G A♭ B♭ C D E♭

E♭ Major Key signature

3♭'s— B♭, E♭ & A♭

Principal chords

E♭ A♭ B♭7

E♭ Major Scale

E♭ F G A♭ B♭ C D E♭

E♭ Major Key signature

3♭'s— B♭, E♭ & A♭

Principal chords

E♭ A♭ B♭7

Key of E Major

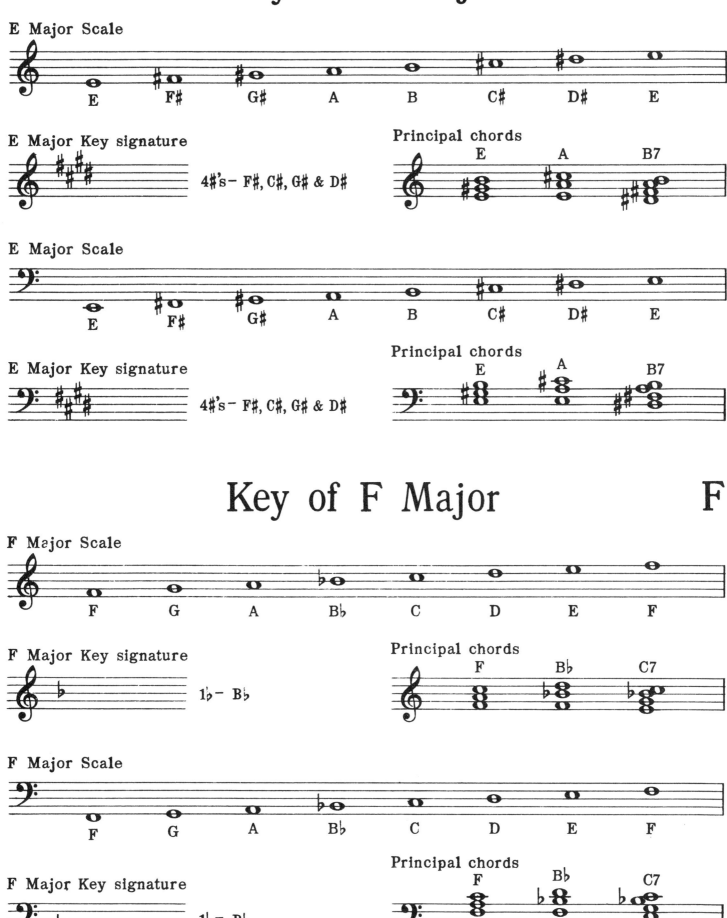

E Major Scale

E F♯ G♯ A B C♯ D♯ E

E Major Key signature

4♯'s – F♯, C♯, G♯ & D♯

Principal chords

E A B7

E Major Scale

E F♯ G♯ A B C♯ D♯ E

E Major Key signature

4♯'s – F♯, C♯, G♯ & D♯

Principal chords

E A B7

Key of F Major

F Major Scale

F G A B♭ C D E F

F Major Key signature

1♭ – B♭

Principal chords

F B♭ C7

F Major Scale

F G A B♭ C D E F

F Major Key signature

1♭ – B♭

Principal chords

F B♭ C7

E

F

F♯
(G♭)

Key of F♯ Major
(Same Sound as Key of G♭ Major with 6 flats)

F♯ Major Scale

F♯   G♯   A♯   B   C♯   D♯   E♯   F♯

F♯ Major Key signature

6♯'s — F♯, C♯, G♯, D♯, A♯ & E♯

Principal chords

F♯   B   C♯7

G♭ Major Key signature

6♭'s — B♭, E♭, A♭, D♭, G♭ & C♭

Principal chords

G♭   C♭   D♭7

F♯ Major Scale

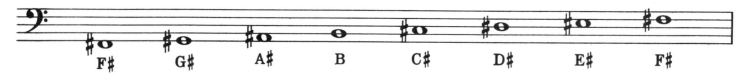

F♯   G♯   A♯   B   C♯   D♯   E♯   F♯

F♯ Major Key signature

6♯'s — F♯, C♯, G♯, D♯, A♯ & E♯

Principal chords

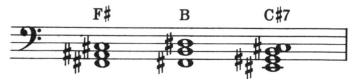

F♯   B   C♯7

G♭ Major Key signature

6♭'s — B♭, E♭, A♭, D♭, G♭ & C♭

Principal chords

G♭   C♭   D♭7

Key of G Major

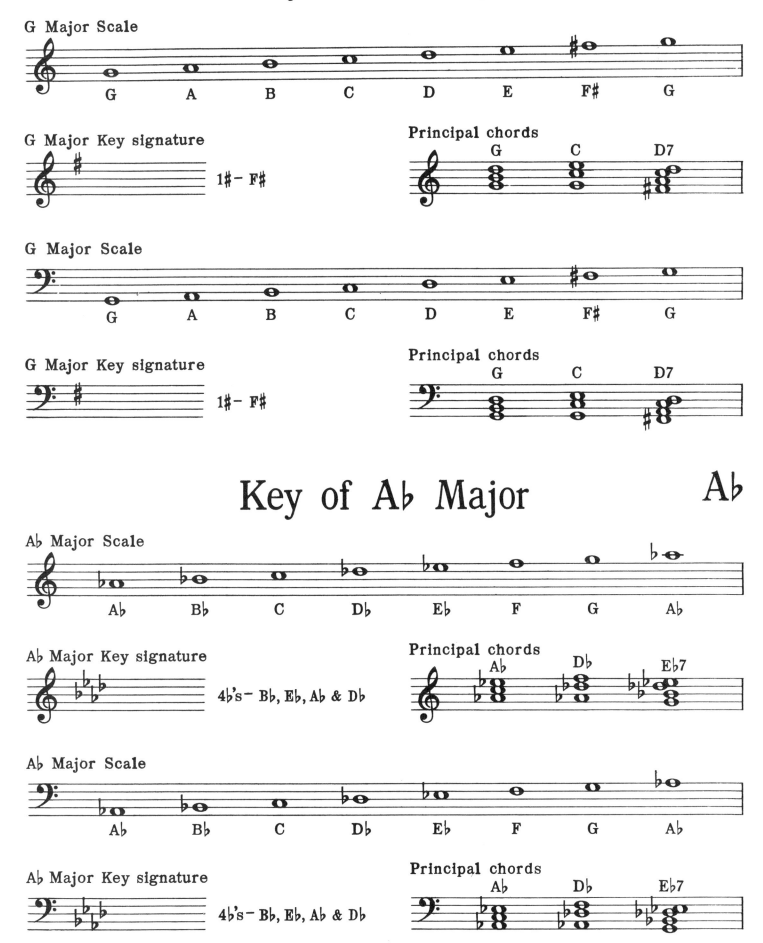

G Major Scale

G   A   B   C   D   E   F#   G

G Major Key signature

1# – F#

Principal chords

G   C   D7

G Major Scale

G   A   B   C   D   E   F#   G

G Major Key signature

1# – F#

Principal chords

G   C   D7

Key of A♭ Major

A♭

A♭ Major Scale

A♭   B♭   C   D♭   E♭   F   G   A♭

A♭ Major Key signature

4♭'s – B♭, E♭, A♭ & D♭

Principal chords

A♭   D♭   E♭7

A♭ Major Scale

A♭   B♭   C   D♭   E♭   F   G   A♭

A♭ Major Key signature

4♭'s – B♭, E♭, A♭ & D♭

Principal chords

A♭   D♭   E♭7

A   Key of A Major

A Major Scale

A   B   C♯   D   E   F♯   G♯   A

A Major Key signature

3♯'s– F♯, C♯ & G♯

Principal chords

A   D   E7

A Major Scale

A   B   C♯   D   E   F♯   G♯   A

A Major Key signature

3♯'s– F♯, C♯ & G♯

Principal chords

A   D   E7

B♭   Key of B♭ Major

B♭ Major Scale

B♭   C   D   E♭   F   G   A   B♭

B♭ Major Key signature

2♭'s– B♭ & E♭

Principal chords

B♭   E♭   F7

B♭ Major Scale

B♭   C   D   E♭   F   G   A   B♭

B♭ Major Key signature

2♭'s– B♭ & E♭

Principal chords

B♭   E♭   F7

10

Key of B Major
(Same Sound as Key of C♭ Major with 7 flats)

B Major Scale

B   C   D♯   E   F♯   G♯   A♯   B

B Major Key signature

5♯'s – F♯, C♯, G♯, D♯ & A♯

Principal chords

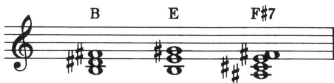

B   E   F♯7

C♭ Major Key signature

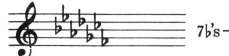

7♭'s – B♭, E♭, A♭, D♭, G♭, C♭ & F♭

Principal chords

C♭   F♭   G♭7

B Major Scale

B   C♯   D♯   E   F♯   G♯   A♯   B

B Major Key signature

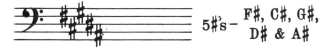

5♯'s – F♯, C♯, G♯, D♯ & A♯

Principal chords

B   E   F♯7

C♭ Major Key signature

7♭'s – B♭, E♭, A♭, D♭, G♭, C♭ & F♭

Principal chords

C♭   F♭   G♭7

TREBLE CLEF CHORDS

BASS CLEF CHORDS

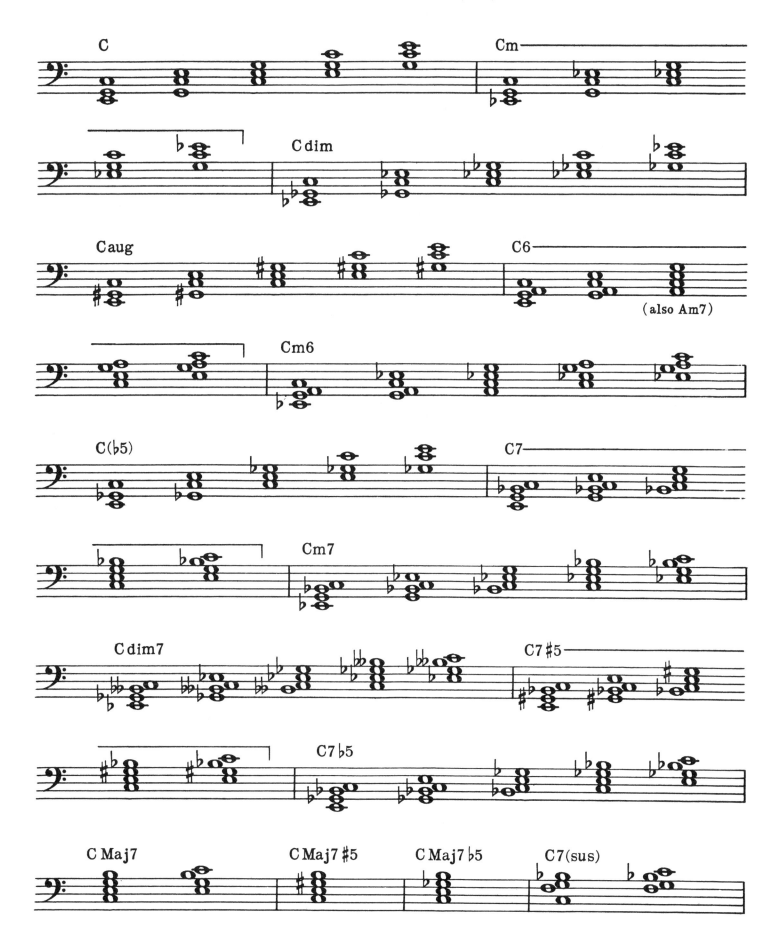

CHORDS FOR BOTH HANDS

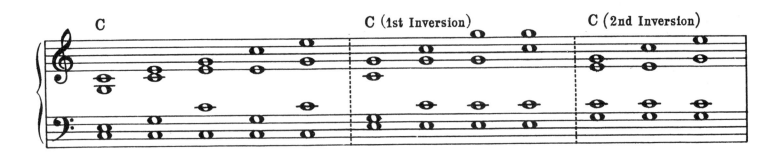

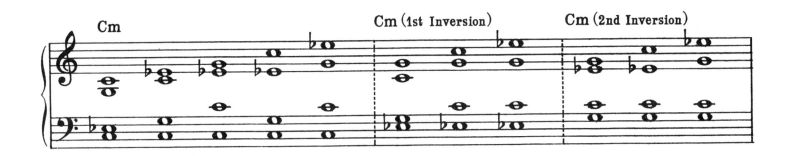

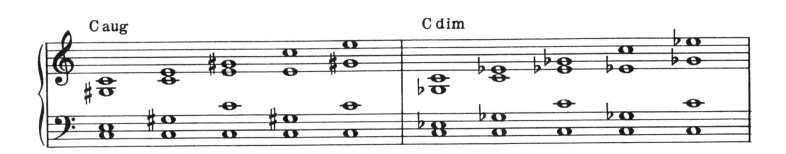

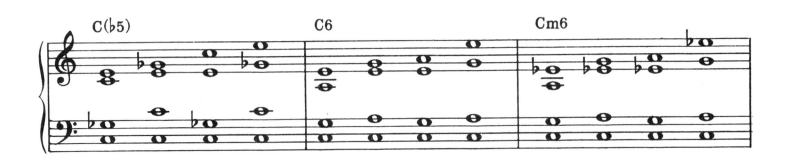

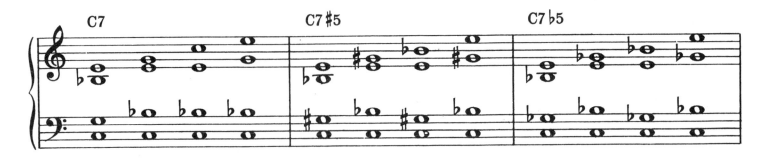

C

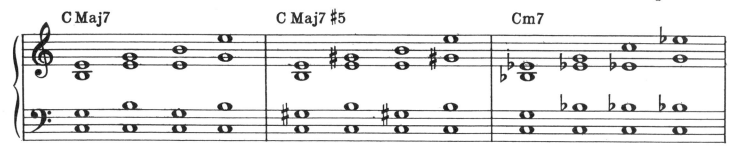

C Maj7   C Maj7 ♯5   Cm7

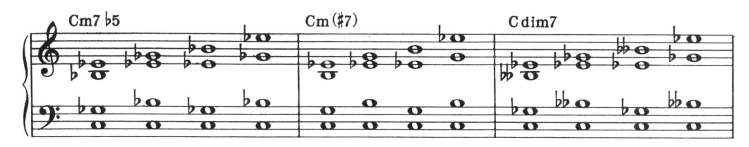

Cm7 ♭5   Cm(♯7)   Cdim7

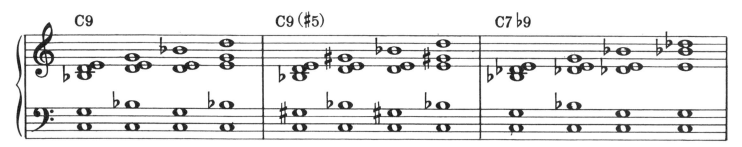

C9   C9 (♯5)   C7 ♭9

C9 (♭5)   C7 (sus)   C7 ♯5 ♭9   C7 ♯9   C7 ♯5 ♯9

Cm9   Cm9 ♭5   C Maj7 (add 9)   C11   C13

C13 (2nd Form)   C13 (♭9)   C13 (♯11)   C aug11   C6/9   Cm6/9

TREBLE CLEF CHORDS

BASS CLEF CHORDS

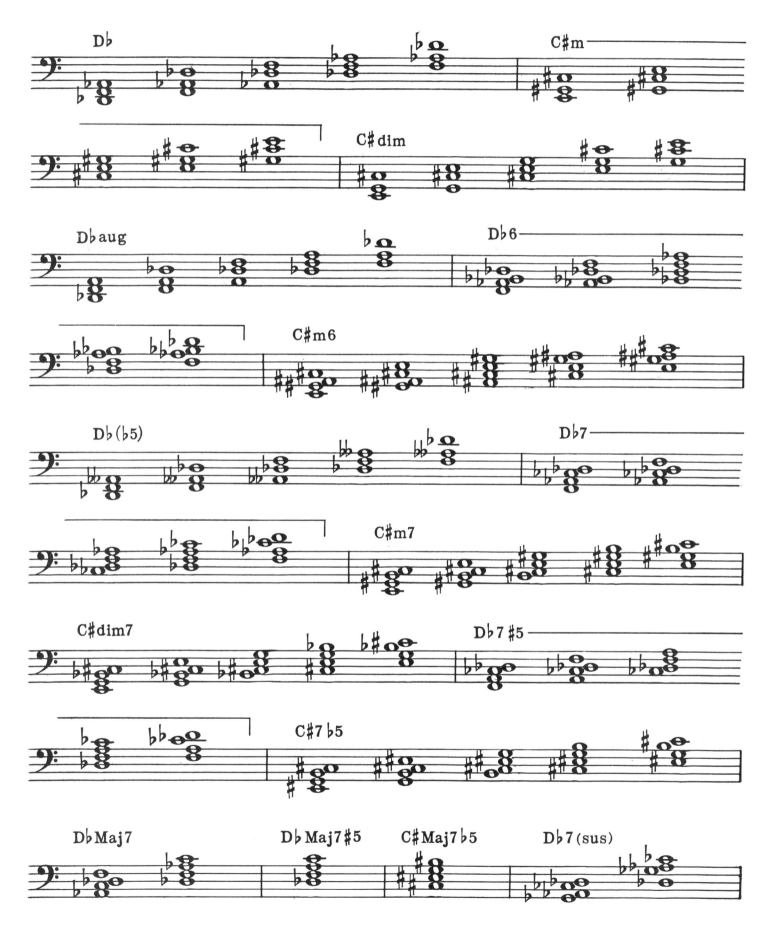

Db
(C#)

CHORDS FOR BOTH HANDS

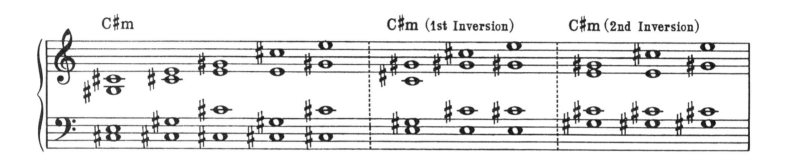

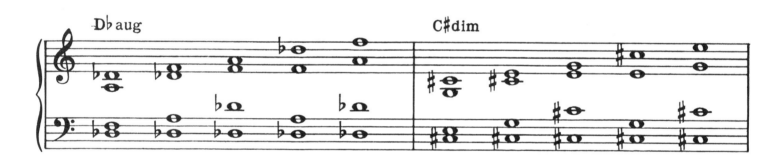

𝄞𝄢 : **D♭**
(C#)

Db Maj7   Db Maj7 #5   C#m7

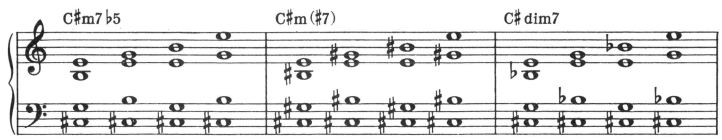

C#m7 b5   C#m (#7)   C# dim7

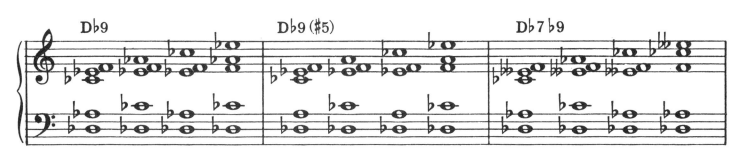

Db9   Db9 (#5)   Db7 b9

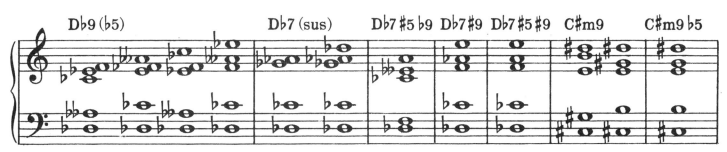

Db9 (b5)   Db7 (sus)   Db7 #5 b9   Db7 #9   Db7 #5 #9   C#m9   C#m9 b5

Db Maj7 (add 9)   Db11   Db13   Db13 (2nd Form)

Db13 (b9)   Db13 (#11)   Db aug11   Db6/9   C#m6/9

D

TREBLE CLEF CHORDS

BASS CLEF CHORDS

D 𝄞 𝄢 CHORDS FOR BOTH HANDS

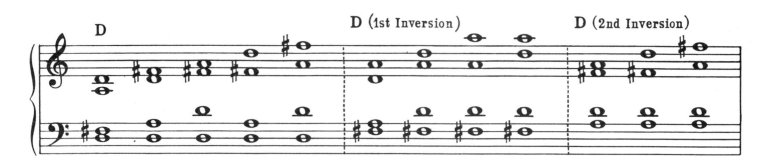

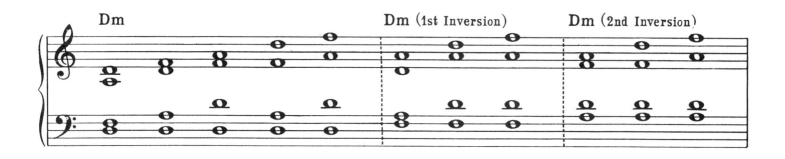

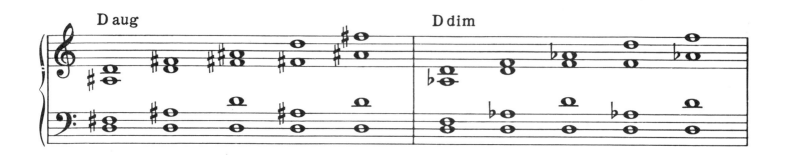

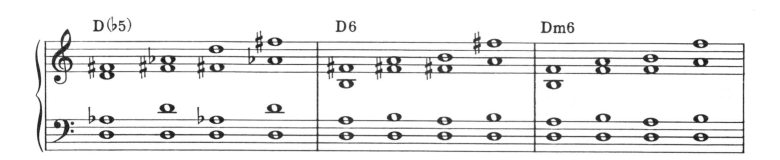

TREBLE CLEF CHORDS

BASS CLEF CHORDS

CHORDS FOR BOTH HANDS

E♭ 𝄞|𝄢

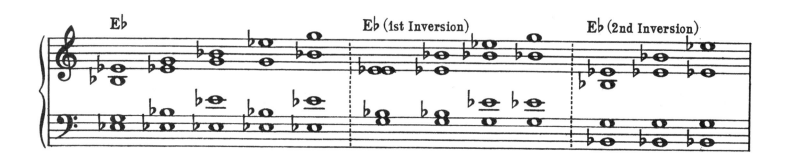

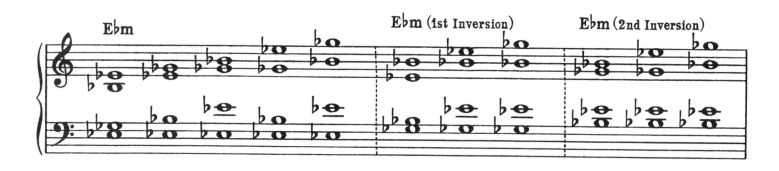

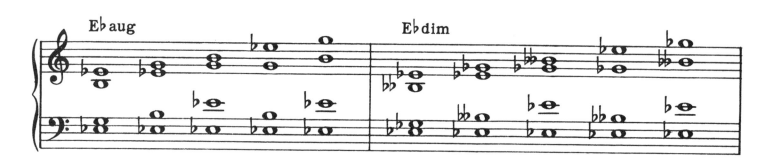

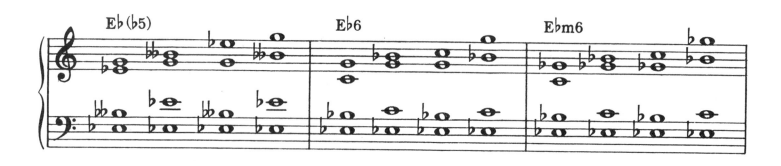

26

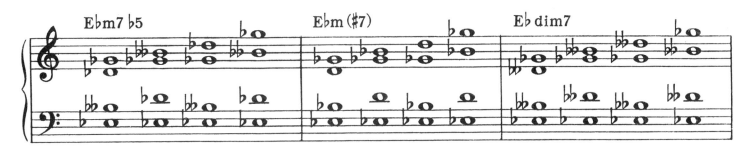

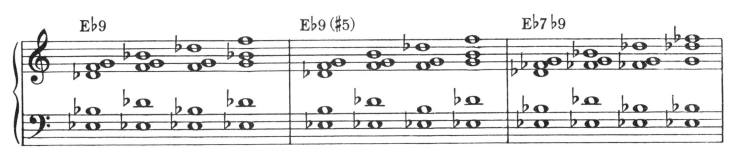

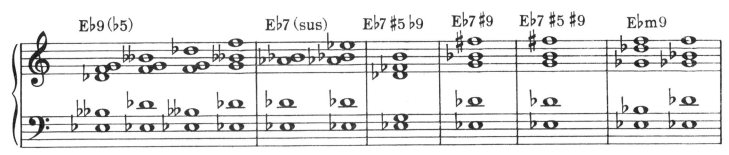

TREBLE CLEF CHORDS

BASS CLEF CHORDS

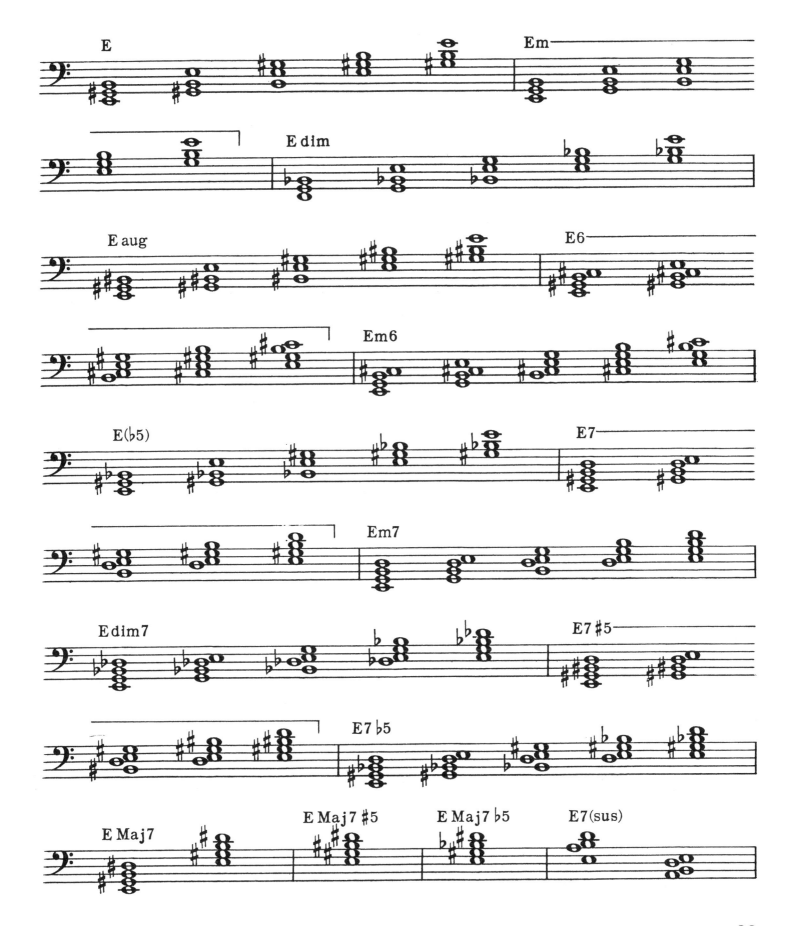

BOTH HANDS

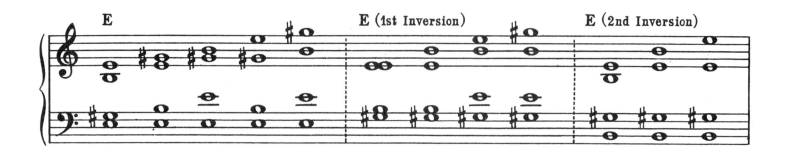

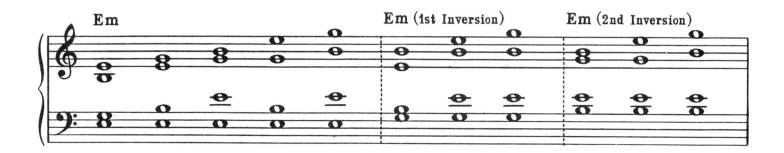

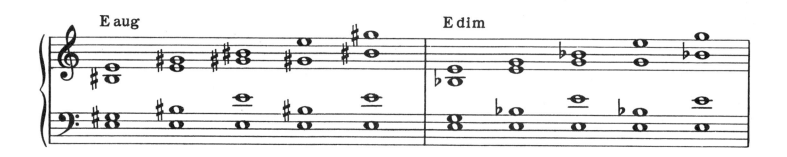

TREBLE CLEF CHORDS

BASS CLEF CHORDS

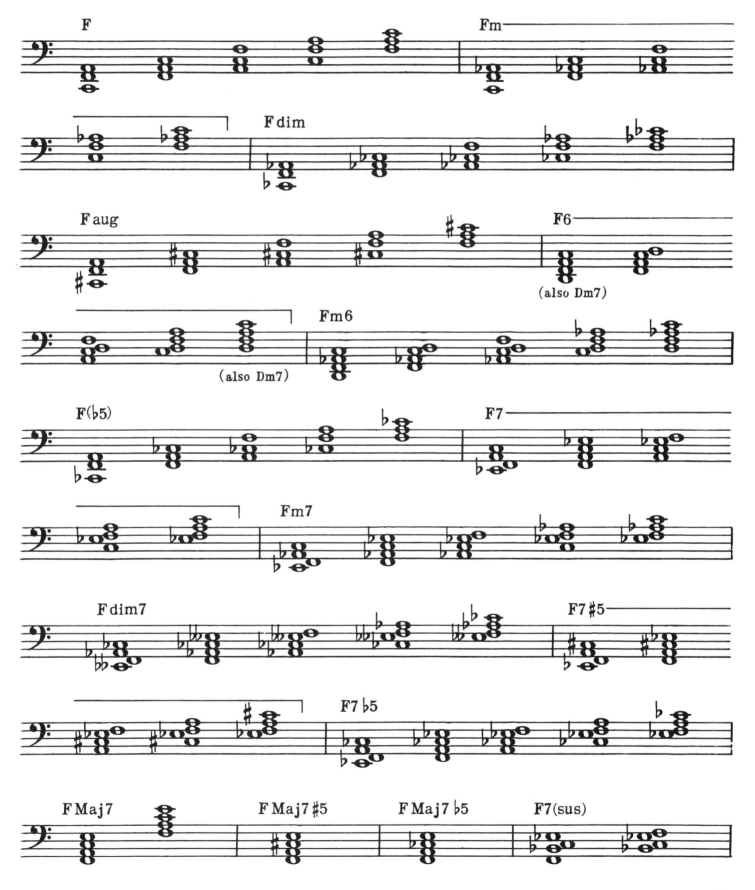

CHORDS FOR BOTH HANDS

F

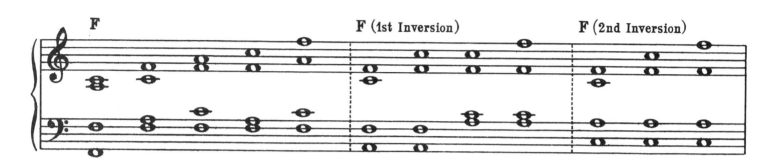

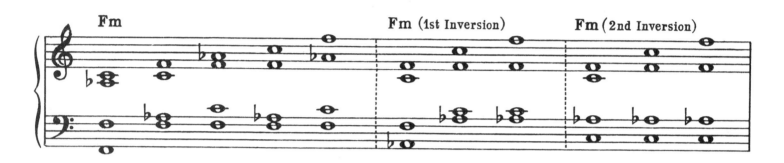

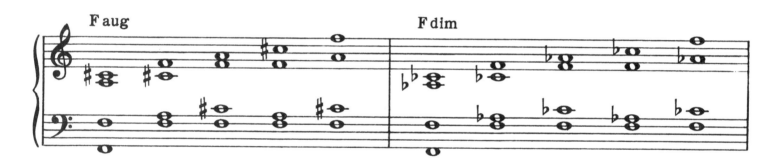

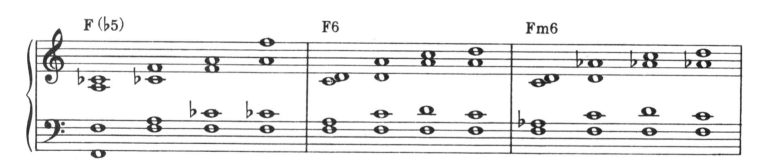

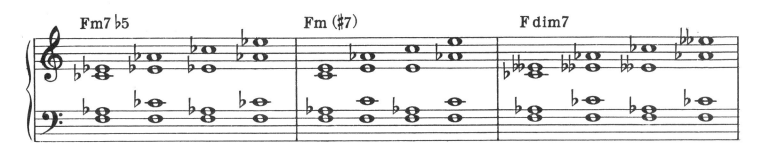

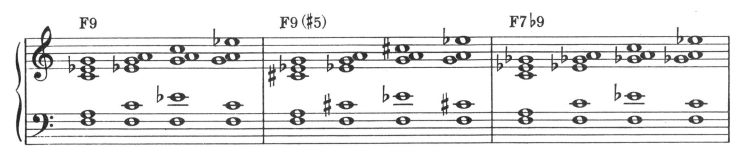

TREBLE CLEF CHORDS

BASS CLEF CHORDS

(G♭)

CHORDS FOR BOTH HANDS

F# Maj7   G♭ Maj7 #5   F#m7

F#m7 ♭5   F#m (#7)   F#dim7

F#9   G♭9 (#5)   F#7 ♭9

F#9 ♭5   F#7 (sus)   G♭7 #5 ♭9   G♭7 #9   G♭7 #5 #9   F#m9

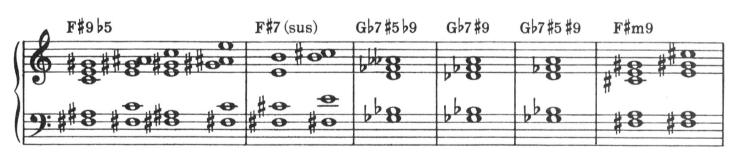

F#m9 ♭5   F# Maj7 (add 9)   F#11   F#13

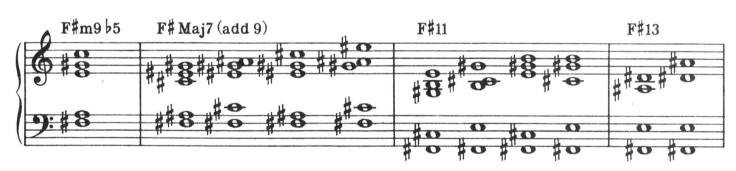

F#13 (2nd Form)   F#13 (♭9)   F#13 (#11)   F# aug11   F#6/9   F#m6/9

TREBLE CLEF CHORDS

BASS CLEF CHORDS

CHORDS FOR BOTH HANDS

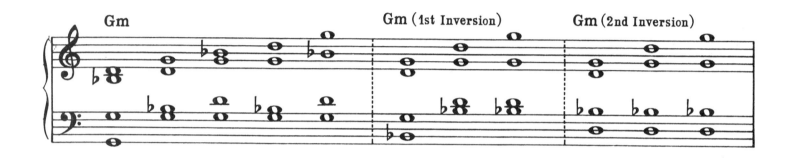

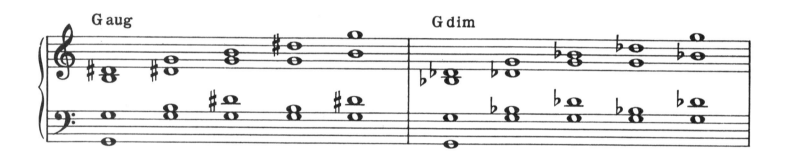

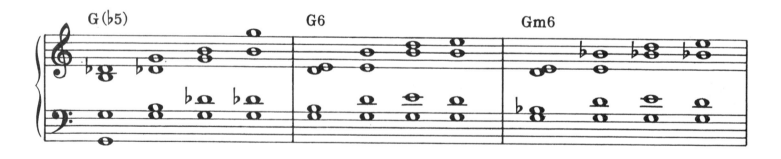

G Maj7 · G Maj7 #5 · Gm7

Gm7♭5 · Gm(♯7) · G dim7

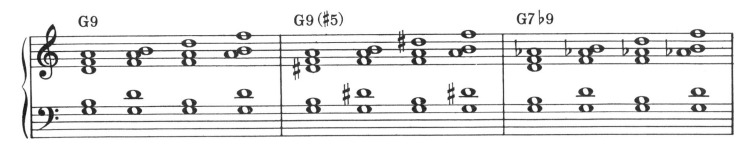

G9 · G9(♯5) · G7♭9

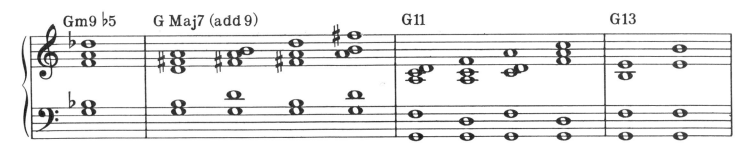

G9(♭5) · G7(sus) · G7 ♯5 ♭9 · G7(♯9) · G7 ♯5 ♯9 · Gm9

Gm9♭5 · G Maj7(add 9) · G11 · G13

G13 (2nd Form) · G13(♭9) · G13(♯11) · G aug 11 · G6/9 · Gm6/9

TREBLE CLEF CHORDS

(also Fm7)

BASS CLEF CHORDS

Ab 𝄞𝄢 CHORDS FOR BOTH HANDS

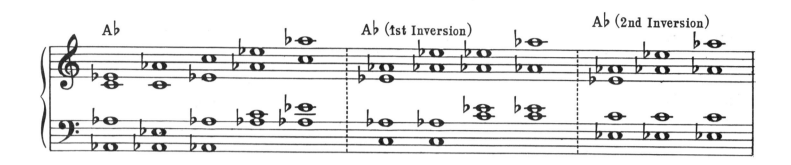

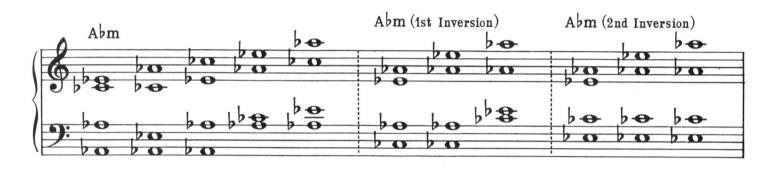

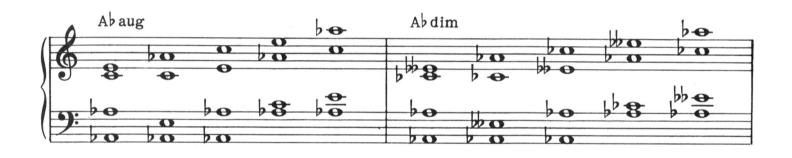

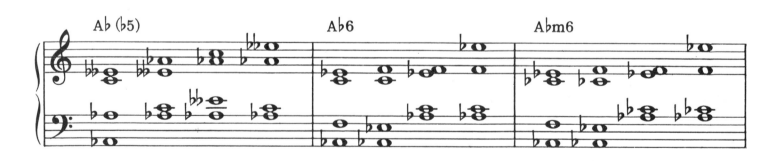

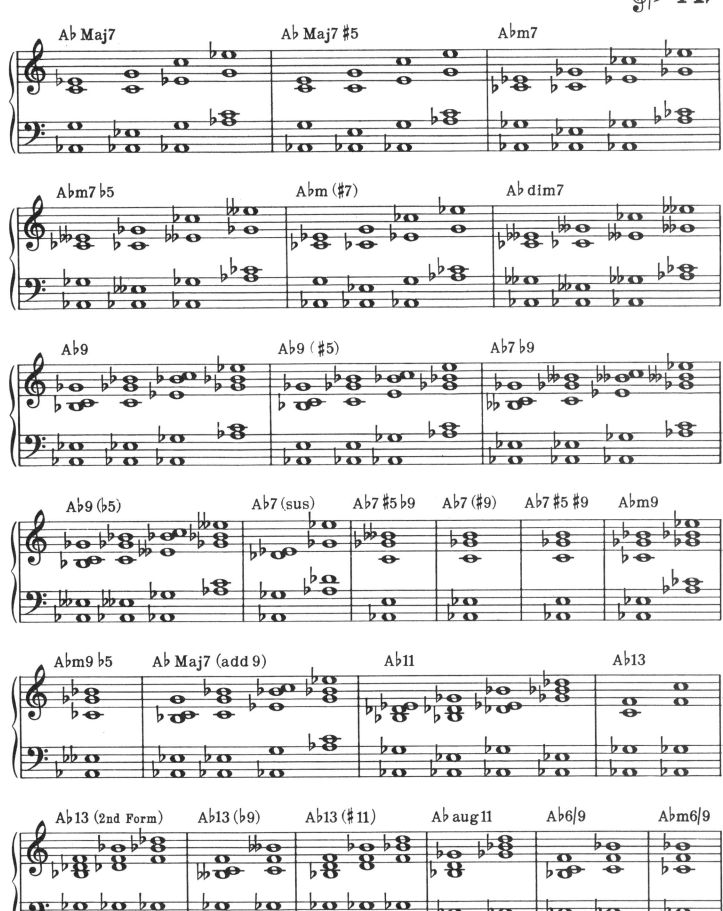

TREBLE CLEF CHORDS

BASS CLEF CHORDS

A 𝄞𝄢 CHORDS FOR BOTH HANDS

A   A (1st Inversion)   A (2nd Inversion)

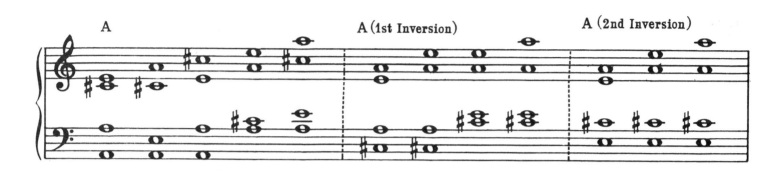

Am   Am (1st Inversion)   Am (2nd Inversion)

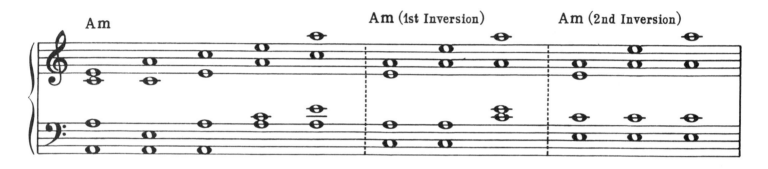

A aug   A dim

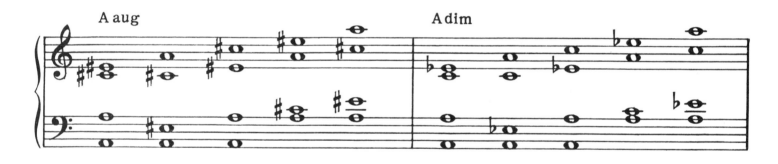

A(♭5)   A6   Am6

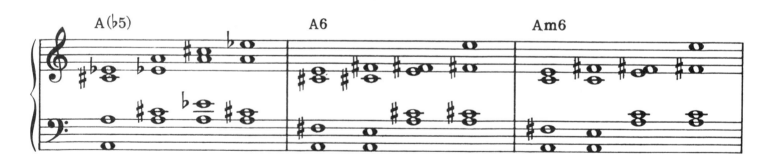

A7   A7 ♯5   A7 ♭5

A Maj7   A Maj7 ♯5   Am7

Am7 ♭5   Am (♯7)   A dim7

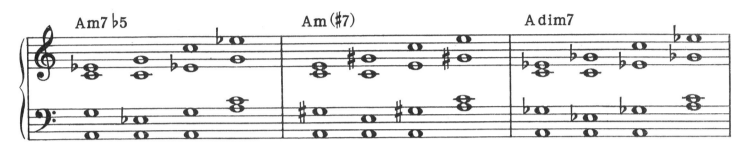

A9   A9 (♯5)   A7 ♭9

A9 (♭5)   A7 (sus)   A7 ♯5 ♭9   A7 (♯9)   A7 ♯5 ♯9   Am9

Am9 ♭5   A Maj7 (add 9)   A11   A13

A13 (2nd Form)   A13 (♭9)   A13 (♯11)   A aug 11   A6/9   Am6/9

TREBLE CLEF CHORDS

BASS CLEF CHORDS

CHORDS FOR BOTH HANDS

B♭ 𝄞 𝄢

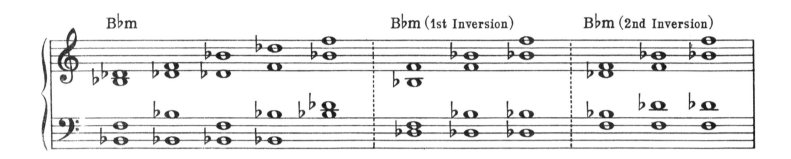

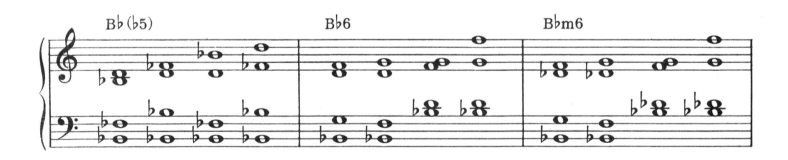

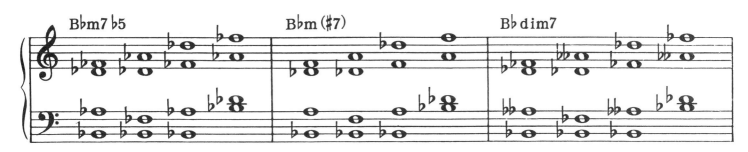

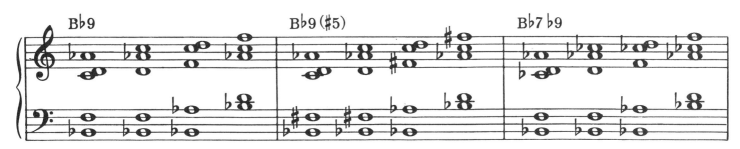

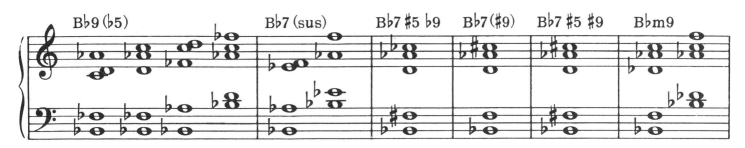

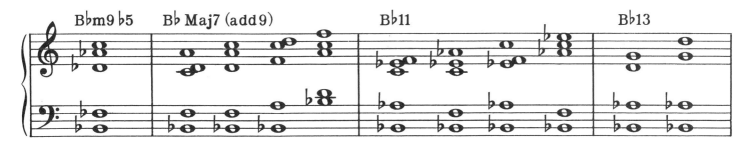

TREBLE CLEF CHORDS

BASS CLEF CHORDS

(also G#m7)

57

CHORDS FOR BOTH HANDS

B
(C♭)

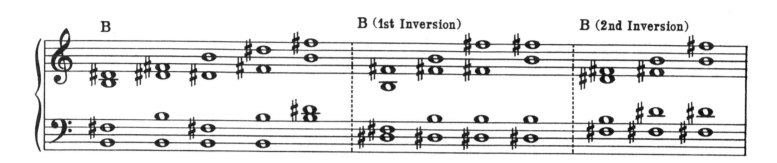

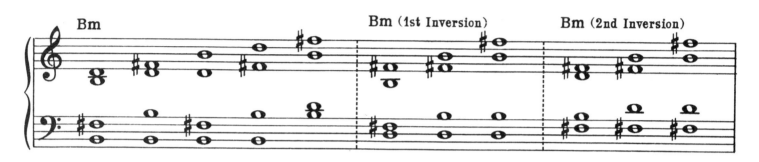

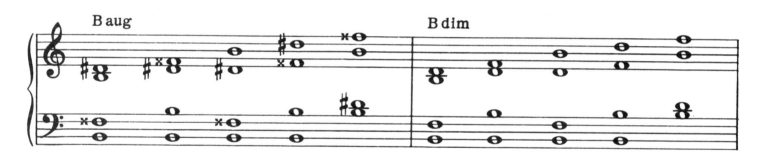

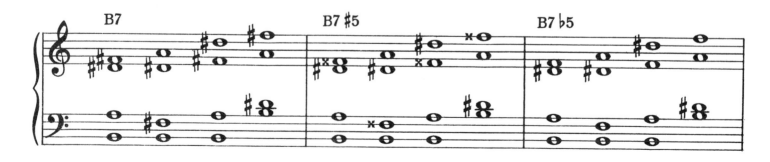

B Maj7 · B Maj7 #5 · Bm7

Bm7 b5 · Bm (#7) · B dim7

B9 (b5) · B9 (#5) · B7 b9

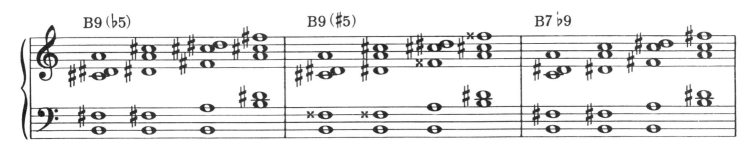

B9 (b5) · B7 (sus) · B7 #5 b9 · B7 (#9) · B7 #5 #9 · Bm9

Bm9 b5 · B Maj7 (add 9) · B11 · B13

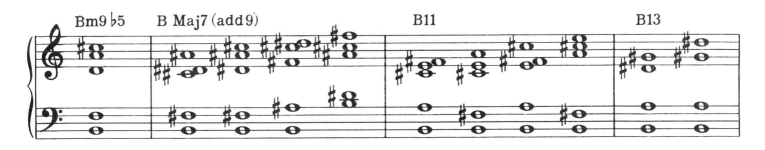

B13 (2nd Form) · B13 (b9) · B13 (#11) · B aug 11 · B6/9 · Bm6/9

Chords for Organ

C-D♭ ORGAN
(C#)

In certain chords the spelling has been altered in order to facilitate reading. For clarity, try the chords with a pure flute stop.

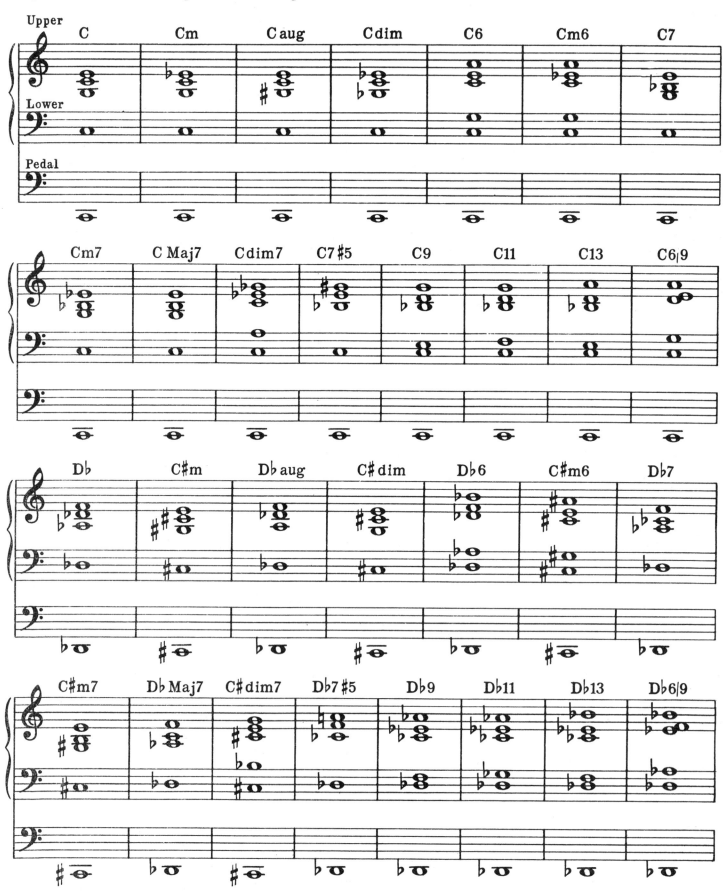

60

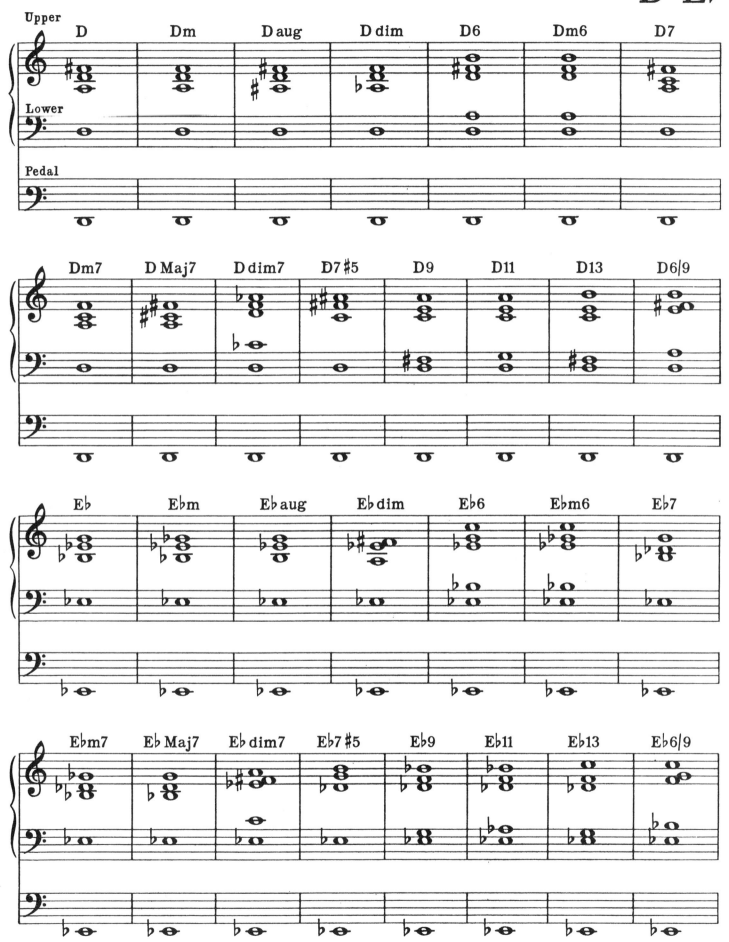

E-F ORGAN

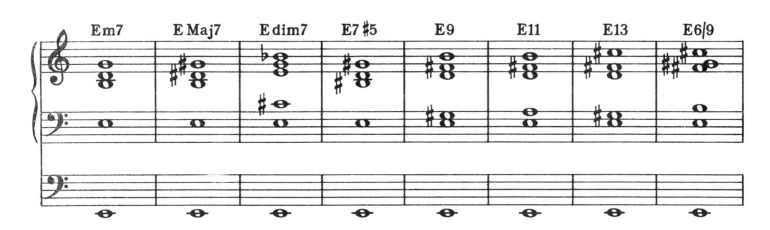

A♭–A ORGAN

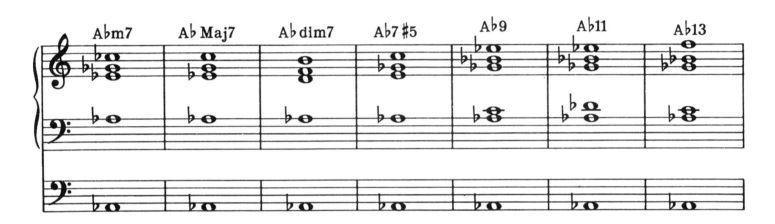